STORIES FROM THE BIBLE

THE OLD TESTAMENT

First published in this edition in 2007 by Evans Brothers Ltd.,
2A Portman Mansions, Chiltern St, London W1U 6NR

Created and produced by Rachel Coombs, Nicholas Harris, Sarah
Hartley and Erica Simms, Orpheus Books Ltd.

Text by Olivia Brookes

Consultant: Robert Willoughby, London School of Theology, Middlesex,
England

Illustrated by Nicki Palin

ISBN 978-0-237534-57-8

Printed and bound in China.

Evans

British Library Cataloguing in Publication Data

Brookes, Olivia
    The Old Testament. - (Stories from the Bible)
    1. Bible stories, English - O.T - Juvenile literature
    I. Title II. Palin, Nicki
    221.9'505

ISBN-13: 9780237534578

STORIES FROM THE BIBLE

THE OLD TESTAMENT

Illustrated by Nicki Palin

Evans

Contents

Introduction

BIBLE STORIES have been told to people young and old for centuries. The stories selected in these pages are just some of the many tales from the first chapters of the Bible, known as the Old Testament to Christians and the Hebrew Bible to Jews. Read about the lives of prophets and ordinary people who embarked on extraordinary journeys for their faith. You will learn why Adam and Eve were cast out of the Garden of Eden, how David beat Goliath in battle and how Jonah found himself inside a whale's belly.

The Garden of Eden

GOD created Adam and Eve. They lived in a beautiful place called the Garden of Eden. They were allowed to eat anything in the garden except for fruit from the Tree of Knowledge of Good and Evil. God said they would die if they ate this fruit. One day Eve was tempted by a snake to disobey God's command. The snake told her she would not die, but would gain knowledge of good and evil. So she and Adam ate the fruit. When God found out, He cast them out of the Garden.

Noah's ark

IN THE years after Adam and Eve were expelled from the Garden of Eden, God saw that men and women had grown increasingly wicked. Only one man, Noah, lived a good life. So God decided to send a great flood and destroy all living things on the Earth. God would save Noah along with his family. God told him to build an ark, a huge wooden boat with many compartments, and stock it with plenty of food. Noah and his family would live on the ark with one pair of each animal species when the rains came. These rains would flood the Earth. Only the people and animals afloat on the ark would survive.

F OR FORTY days and forty nights, it rained. The flood waters rose. All living things were drowned, save Noah and the inhabitants of the ark. Eventually, the rain stopped. Noah sent a dove to find land. When the dove came back with an olive branch, he knew that it would soon be safe to leave the ark. God told Noah to repopulate the Earth. Noah gave thanks to God. A rainbow appeared across the sky. It was a symbol of God's promise never to destroy the Earth again.

Abraham and Jacob

IN THE CITY of Haran lived a man called Abram. One day God told Abram to leave Haran and go to Canaan. There he would become the father of a great nation. His descendants would be as numerous as the stars. Abram and his wife, Sarai, were very old but God gave them a son, Isaac. God told Abram to change his name to Abraham—"father of many"—and his wife's name to Sarah as a sign of His promise to give them a son.

GOD decided to test Abraham's faith. Abraham was to take his only son, Isaac, and offer him as a sacrifice. Abraham loved his son very much but he did as God asked. He bound Isaac and placed him on an altar. But, as he raised his knife, an angel appeared and told him to stop. Abraham had passed the test. Seeing a ram caught in a bush, Abraham sacrificed the animal instead.

ISAAC married Rebekah. They had two sons, Esau and Jacob. Later in life, Isaac became blind. Jacob tricked his father into thinking he was the elder child. He was given the blessing intended for Esau. When Esau found out, Jacob was forced to flee.

On his way to Haran from Beersheba, Jacob had a dream. Angels walked up and down a staircase reaching up to heaven. God spoke to him. He promised Jacob that the place where he slept would be saved for his children. Jacob called the place Bethel, meaning "House of God."

Joseph

J ACOB had many children. His favourite son was called Joseph, son
of Rachel. On Joseph's seventeenth birthday, Jacob gave him a
present: a coat with long sleeves. It was woven with many different
coloured threads into elaborate patterns. Joseph's eleven brothers
resented Joseph because their father thought of him as his heir, even
though he was not the eldest.

ONE DAY, Jacob asked Joseph to check on his brothers, who were herding sheep. When his brothers saw Joseph in the distance they knew he had been sent to check on them, so they plotted against him. They decided to throw him down a well where he would starve to death. But, as they lowered him down, some merchants arrived. Joseph's brothers decided to sell him to the merchants instead. Then they took his coat back to Jacob and told him that his favourite son had been killed.

Joseph in Egypt

JOSEPH was taken to Egypt and sold as a slave to Potiphar, an official. Two years later, Pharaoh had a troubling dream. Seven thin cows ate seven fat ones, but they did not grow fatter. None of his advisors could tell him what the dream meant. Joseph had accurately interpreted the dreams of two of Pharaoh's servants before, so Pharaoh sent for Joseph. Joseph told Pharaoh that his dream was a warning. There would be seven years of good crops and seven years of famine. He advised Pharaoh to collect food now so he could feed his people later.

PHARAOH was so impressed that he put Joseph in charge of the grain stores. Eventually, Joseph became a governor of Egypt. But, back home in Canaan, Jacob and his family were starving. Jacob sent his sons to Egypt to find food. They arrived at Joseph's house but did not recognize him. Joseph sold them grain but told them to return with their youngest brother, Benjamin. When they came back, Joseph devised a plan to force Benjamin to stay in Egypt. He secretly hid a silver goblet in Benjamin's sack. When it was later "found", Joseph ordered that Benjamin be arrested. Another brother, Judah, pleaded with Joseph to release Benjamin. Joseph now saw his brothers were changed men, so he told them who he was. The brothers were overjoyed. Pharaoh told Joseph to invite his family to live in Egypt. Jacob was delighted to see his long-lost son.

Moses

MOSES was born in troubled times. Pharaoh thought there were too many Israelites in Egypt. He ordered that all Israelites would become slaves and that all Israelite baby boys were to be put to death. When he was a baby, Moses's mother kept him hidden for a long time, but as he grew she realised that he, an Israelite, was no longer safe with her. She made a basket from papyrus and hid her child among the reeds on the River Nile. The basket was discovered by Pharaoh's daughter. She and her maids raised Moses as an Egyptian prince.

MOSES knew that the Egyptians treated their slaves badly. He was so angry at seeing an Israelite slave beaten that he killed the Egyptian man responsible. He fled to Midan and became a shepherd. One day a nearby bush burst into flames. God called to him from the flames. He told Moses to go back to Egypt and tell Pharaoh to set the slaves free.

WHEN Pharaoh refused, God sent ten plagues. The Nile water turned into blood. There were swarms of gnats, flies, frogs and locusts. People were covered in boils and their livestock died. Hail destroyed their crops and there was darkness for three days. God told Moses that every first-born child in Egypt would die. But if the Israelites marked their houses with lamb's blood, their children would be unharmed.

The Exodus

I N HIS ANGER Pharaoh ordered the Israelites to leave Egypt immediately. But he soon regretted the loss of his prized slaves and sent his army to bring them back. The Israelites reached the Red Sea when Pharaoh's chariots caught up with them. The Israelites were trapped. God told Moses to stretch out his hand over the sea. He did so and the waters parted. They walked to safety.

T HE EGYPTIAN chariots tried to follow but, as they reached the sea bed, Moses stretched out his hand once more and the waters came crashing down. The Egyptians were drowned and the Israelites continued on their journey into the desert.

WHEN their food ran out, the Israelites complained to Moses. The next morning the ground was covered with flakes called manna that tasted of honey. Moses struck a rock and water began to flow out. God told Moses that the Israelites must have faith and take only enough food for one day. He would provide more each day.

THE Israelites reached Mount Sinai. They made camp while Moses climbed to the top. God gave him Ten Commandments, laws that the Israelites were to obey. Moses carved them on two stone tablets. When Moses returned to the camp he saw the people worshipping a statue of a golden calf. They said it was the god that led them out of Egypt. Moses was horrified. In his anger, he smashed the tablets and destroyed the calf. But God instructed Moses to cut two new tablets.

Joshua

WHEN Moses died, God chose Joshua to be his successor. God told Joshua that as long as he lived no one would stand in his way. All the Israelite tribes accepted Joshua as their leader and promised to obey him as they had obeyed Moses. Joshua was to lead the Israelites into Canaan, the land that had been promised to Abraham. But Canaan was already ruled by several kings. To conquer the land for the Israelites, Joshua would have to defeat all their armies. Joshua gathered his men together and they prepared to go into battle. As he led them across the River Jordan, the waters dried up.

JOSHUA'S army approached Jericho, a fortress city in Canaan. The people of Jericho barricaded themselves behind its walls. But God gave Joshua instructions on how to conquer the city. Joshua marched his men once around the walls each day for six days. At the front of the procession, seven priests carried seven trumpets in front of the Ark of the Covenant, the chest containing the tablets inscribed with the Ten Commandments.

ON THE seventh day, they marched around Jericho seven times. On the last lap, the priests blew their trumpets. Then the Israelites shouted a mighty war cry and the walls of Jericho began to crumble and fall to the ground. The Israelites stormed the city and destroyed it. Joshua then placed a curse on anyone who tried to rebuild Jericho.

Samson and Delilah

FOR MANY YEARS, the Israelites fought against the Philistines. God decided to bless a childless Israelite couple with a son who would one day stand up to the Philistines. Samson grew up to be incredibly strong. His strength was in his hair, which had never been cut. He fell in love with a Philistine woman called Delilah, who tricked him into telling her the secret of his strength. She cut off his hair and handed him over to the Philistines. Samson's strength was gone. The Philistines blinded him and imprisoned him in Gaza. While he was in prison, Samson's hair began to grow back. He prayed to God to give him strength.

THE PHILISTINES held a celebration in praise of their god, Dagon, to thank him for helping them defeat Samson. They took Samson from prison so they could mock him. Samson asked the boy who was leading him to lean him against the pillars of the temple so he could rest. He cried out to God asking for His help. Then he pushed against the two main pillars of the building. His strength had returned and the temple collapsed. But Samson was crushed to death, along with all the Philistines who were gathered there.

Samuel

WHEN Samuel was a boy, he went to study with Eli, a priest in the temple at Jerusalem. One night, he woke to hear someone calling his name. He ran to Eli but the priest had not called him. After this had happened several times, the priest understood that it was God calling to Samuel. He told the boy to listen to what God was trying to tell him. So Samuel listened and God made him His prophet.

SAMUEL called the Israelites to gather at Mizpah. Here they fasted while Samuel prepared a sacrifice. Meanwhile the Philistine army prepared to attack them. Terrified, the Israelites wanted to fight back but Samuel told them to wait. He called to God and God sent a thunder-clap so loud the Philistines fell to the ground in agony. They never attacked again in Samuel's lifetime.

THE PEOPLE of Israel asked Samuel to choose them a king. God told Samuel that a man would come seeking his help. This man was to be king. Months later, a man called Saul asked Samuel to help him find his lost donkeys. Samuel knew that Saul was God's choice and he anointed him with oil.

BUT SAUL disobeyed God after victory in battle. So God sent Samuel to find a successor. Samuel went to Bethlehem where he was to find the sons of Jesse. One of them was to be the new king. But, as each son came for a blessing, God rejected them. Finally David arrived from the fields where he had been working. God told Samuel this was the one and Samuel anointed him. David was to become the future king of Israel.

David and Goliath

A MIGHTY Philistine warrior named Goliath was terrifying the Israelite army. He challenged the Israelites to a single combat with their finest warrior. Only David was brave enough to accept the challenge. He was armed with just a sling and five stones. Goliath laughed when he saw the young boy. But God was on David's side and Goliath was defeated by a single stone from David's sling.

WHEN Saul died, David became king. To show his thanks to God, David held a great festival and paraded the Ark of the Covenant through the streets of Jerusalem. David was a good king but he was not faultless. He fell in love with Bathsheba. Though she was married to one of his soldiers, Uriah, David slept with her and she became pregnant. David tried to make Uriah believe he had fathered the child himself. The plan failed, so David ordered that Uriah be killed.

Solomon

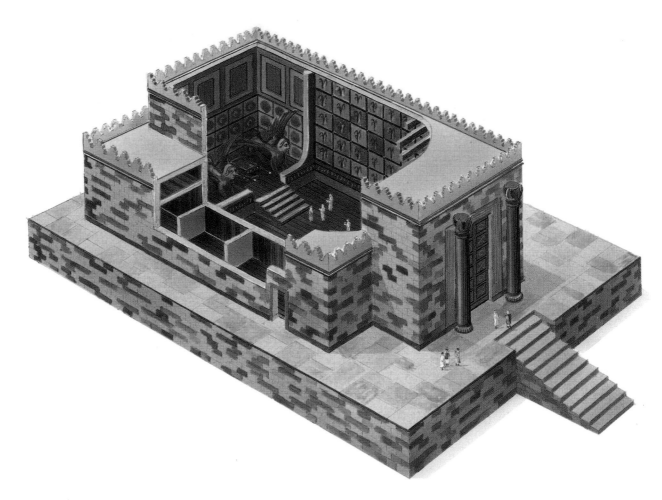

DAVID and Bathsheba's first child died because of the sin David had committed. Their second son, Solomon, became the next king of Israel.

Solomon built a magnificent temple in Jerusalem to house the Ark of the Covenant. It was also a place where the Israelites could go to worship God. The temple took seven years to build. It was made from stone, cedar wood, bronze and gold. Inside, two winged angels guarded the Ark. The walls were covered with gold flowers.

KING SOLOMON was known for his wisdom and commitment to God. He was a diplomat and preferred negotiations and agreements to war.

Solomon's fame reached the Queen of Sheba and she travelled from southern Arabia to meet him. She wanted to test his wisdom. The Queen asked him many difficult questions but Solomon had a clear answer to every one of them. The Queen was very impressed with Solomon's wisdom and the temple he had built. To show her admiration she gave Solomon a special kind of wood to use in the temple as well as gold, spices and precious stones.

In exile

GOD commanded the prophet Jonah to preach to the pagan people of the Assyrian city of Nineveh. But Jonah tried to escape from this task by sailing in the opposite direction. So God sent a whale that swallowed Jonah whole. He remained inside the whale's belly until he repented. The whale then spat him out on to dry land. Jonah went to Nineveh. All the people he spoke to turned to God.

DANIEL was exiled to Babylon when he was just a teenager. He became a high-ranking official in Babylon and later the Persian Empire. He proved to King Cyrus of Persia that the idols the Persians worshipped were not gods. Jealous officials plotted against Daniel. They persuaded King Darius, Cyrus's successor, to throw Daniel into a pit of lions because he would not deny his faith in God. But Daniel prayed to God and was saved.

THE PROPHET Ezekiel was exiled to Babylon. Here he spoke to the people about his visions. In one, he saw a valley of dry bones come back to life as a great army. He explained that this meant that God would give hope back to the Israelites and they would return home.

Index